Post Subject

AKRON SERIES IN POETRY

D1082413

AKRON SERIES IN POETRY
Mary Biddinger, Editor

Oliver de la Paz, *Post Subject: A Fable*
John Repp, *Fat Jersey Blues*
Emilia Phillips, *Signaletics*
Seth Abramson, *Thievery*
Steve Kistulentz, *Little Black Daydream*
Jason Bredle, *Carnival*
Emily Rosko, *Prop Rockery*
Alison Pelegrin, *Hurricane Party*
Matthew Guenette, *American Busboy*
Joshua Harmon, *Le Spleen de Poughkeepsie*
David Dodd Lee, *Orphan, Indiana*
Sarah Perrier, *Nothing Fatal*
Oliver de la Paz, *Requiem for the Orchard*
Rachel Dilworth, *The Wild Rose Asylum*
John Minczeski, *A Letter to Serafin*
John Gallaher, *Map of the Folded World*
Heather Derr-Smith, *The Bride Minaret*
William Greenway, *Everywhere at Once*
Brian Brodeur, *Other Latitudes*

Titles published since 2008.
For a complete listing of titles published in the
series, go to www.uakron.edu/uapress/poetry

Post Subject
A Fable

Oliver de la Paz

The University of Akron Press
Akron, Ohio

18   17   16   15   14   5   4   3   2   1

ISBN: 978-1-937378-88-2 (cloth)
ISBN: 978-1-937378-89-9 (paper)
ISBN: 978-1-629220-08-6 (ePDF)
ISBN: 978-1-629220-09-3 (ePub)

LIBRARY OF CONGRESS CATALOGING-IN-PUBLICATION DATA

De la Paz, Oliver, 1972–

Post subject : a fable / Oliver de la Paz. — First edition.

    pages cm. — (Akron series in poetry)

ISBN 978-1-937378-88-2 (hardback) — ISBN 978-1-937378-89-9 (paperback) — ISBN 978-1-62922-008-6 (epdf)

I. Title.

PS3554.E114P67 2014

811'.54—dc23

2014020387

∞ The paper used in this publication meets the minimum requirements of ANSI/NISO Z39.48–1992 (Permanence of Paper).

Cover: *We All Fall Down* by Matthew Christopher / Abandoned America, copyright (2009), reproduced with permission.

Post Subject was designed and typeset in Bulmer by Amy Freels and printed on sixty-pound natural and bound by Bookmasters of Ashland, Ohio.

ACKNOWLEDGMENTS

Grateful acknowledgments to the following journals where these pieces have appeared, sometimes in different forms and with different titles:

Asian American Literary Review, Barn Owl Review, Codex, The Cossack Review, CURA, The Drunken Boat, Epiphany, Exit 7, Grist, H_NGM_N, Hot Metal Bridge, Kartika Review, Kin, Lantern Review, Many Mountains Moving, Memorious, The Normal School, Painted Bride Quarterly, Pebble Lake Review, Quarter After Eight, and *The Rumpus.*

Many of the poems appeared in *Black Warrior Review* as a chapbook entitled *Post Havoc: A Fable.*

"Dear Empire: [these are your temples]" appears in The Academy of American Poets' *Textflow.*

Contents

Address

These are your ashes   3

Atlas

This is your atoll   7

These are your battlefields   8

These are your boardwalks   9

This is your breeze   10

These are your bridges   11

These are your canyons   12

These are your capitals   13

This is your city   14

These are your countries   15

These are your docks   16

These are your holy places   17

These are your horizons   18

These are your interstates   19

These are your islands   20

These are your maps   21

These are your meadows   22

These are your parks   23

These are your pastures   24

These are your plains   25

These are your salt flats   26

These are your skies   27

These are your springs   28

This is your tremor   29

These are your vistas   30

These are your volcanoes   31

This is your wall   32
These are your wells   33
These are your wires   34

Ledger
This is your aftermath   37
This is your art   38
These are your asylums   39
These are your banners   40
These are your billboards   41
This is your church   42
These are your engines   43
These are your evenings   44
These are your foundries   45
These are your goods   46
These are your guns   47
These are your inquests   48
These are your laws   49
This is your light   50
These are your mercies   51
These are your murders   52
These are your nights   53
These are your orders   54
This is your purview   55
These are your processions   56
This is your product   57
These are your questions   58
These are your radio towers   59
These are your ramparts   60
This is your reliquary   61
This is your sanitarium   62
These are your spires   63

These are your squares 64

These are your structures 65

These are your temples 66

This is your tomb 67

This is your window 68

These are your winters 69

Zoo

These are your aerialists 73

This is your assembly 74

These are your beasts 75

This is your bestiary 76

These are your birds 77

These are your bondsmen 78

These are your dead 79

These are your devotees 80

These are your dissidents 81

These are your followers 82

These are your hagiographers 83

These are your horses 84

These are your idolaters 85

These are your jellyfish 86

These are your nurseries 87

These are your orators 88

These are your percussionists 89

These are your phantoms 90

These are your rebels 91

These are your refugees 92

These are your revelers 93

This is your rival 94

These are your scholars 95

These are your scribes 96

These are your stables 97

This is your stevedore 98

This is your subject 99

These are your slaves 100

This is your ward 101

These are your witnesses 102

These are your worshippers 103

These are your zebras 104

Zygote
This is your photo 107

. . . history is made by men and women, just as it can also be unmade and rewritten, always with various silence and elisions, always with shapes imposed and disfigurements tolerated.
—Edward W. Said

Gentlemen do not read each other's mail.
—Henry L. Stimson

Address

Dear Empire,

These are your ashes. We've carried them for years in baskets, urns, boxes, and lockets. A fine dust clouds our skies. A lock of your hair is hemmed by a selvedge. The cloth adorns an altar in your finest shrine.

Dear Empire, we are an obedient people. We are intimate beyond death, and anxious for your return. We've kept your letters close to our chests. Dear Empire, our arenas still follow your lead.

Come back from where you dwell. In the days you have left us, we've nothing to do but count the elements: it is not raining. It is raining. A garland of flowers dries on marble.

Atlas

Dear Empire,

This is your atoll. Coral crumbles to the touch. The artist paces along the beaches—delicate and glittering. She walks back and forth talking to herself and finds, trapped in a tide pool, a small jellyfish.

Her body softens as she scoops the animal into a little bowl with salt water. Portions of the animal's body are torn. Portions of it blow and settle. Blow and settle. In each of its four quadrants, a square opens and closes. Its little windows blossom into squares of light.

Sea foam dissolves in small puckers, and as the waters pass over sand, the artist's footprints sink beneath its concavity. "Look," she says. "The tide has risen."

Dear Empire,

These are your battlefields. There are monuments here, the dead atop stone horses with their eyes towards the heavens. Under shadow, the scrawl of graffiti and the hardscape of granite pathways guide foot traffic to the raised hoof of one of your dead generals mounted aloft.

Here, the sun blanches stone, dries lichen into crisp rosettes. Winters, the barren trees lean downward, their branches full of ice as if to bow their heads. No birds.

No other animals except occasional foxes nosing about. So much weight presses this place. The shadows of the statues sink the very ground.

Dear Empire,

These are your boardwalks. The young are tedious as they hurl their lithe bodies through the promenade. From marquee to marquee, their eyes flit. Neon trails emblaze into the backs of their skulls. A dullness, then.

Shouts from the midway ricochet with every ball-bearing sprung from a gun. The young are fastidious, combing back their hairs before every mirror.

And despite the carnival's charm, ambitions spin with the Tilt-a-Whirl into an operatic frenzy. There are no refunds given. There are no guides through the funhouse. The lights curl in the concave mirrors.

Dear Empire,

This is your breeze. The sea is a thousand miles away, yet it crushes us still. Blue trees—blue distances wash up on our doorsteps. Off the coast there is a gauntlet of ships, but I cannot smell them from here.

Your children miss the ocean. They sleep in its absence. Cry out for it. Sometimes out of mischief. Sometimes out of genuine longing.

But longing for such a body is no good for us. There are lights here. And arms to keep us safe. We can do without fickle tides, without the spindrift.

Dear Empire,

These are your bridges. They rise high above the depths. And therefore, they control the depths. Are they a way to avert? A desire or a distance? I'm unsure, though their spires remind me of the backs of sleepers.

Their lateral frames break the stuttering sky, the stuttering water. And therefore, there is no marriage, only a gap. We drive over. Boats pass under the struts, careful not to brush against the sides as a kind of intimacy or love. There is so much love between boats and what touches their hulls.

Your boats. Your bridges. Lazily, through the lattice of girders, the river heads to the sea. Who will love the boats beyond the river but these bridges, their memories, riveted and clean?

Dear Empire,

These are your canyons. They are hollow. Where once there were saguaros, mesas, whole oceans of succulents—now craters carved by artillery.

There are no imminent city vistas, but there are men here who make elegant queues down the curve of the landscape. Their bodies, thin, like the veins on the underside of leaves. They are handsome in their hungers.

I want to take a picture of their faces. I want to hang their faces on my wall to cancel banality. To house their eyes next to the table. To house their cheeks, so sunken and deep.

Dear Empire,

These are your capitals. There's one, high above the desert plains.
From its parapets, you see elephant herds bathe themselves in dust
from dry river beds. And when it rains, the savannah's greenery
descends from the mountains, follows the streams of cold, glacial
waters. Every animal of this desert is yours.

And here is your forest capital, where wolves encircle the timber
portcullis, despite our traps in their dens. From the balconies, you can
hear them rattle the tin shingles of the breezeway.

From both houses, the skies are cast in the glow of your electric works.
There is no more darkness. The stars are masked in your constant dusk.

Dear Empire,

This is your city. Tonight, everything turns to glass. Lights evade a firm story. The lights are beyond their fire—they are the condition:

First condition: contour and shadow. The flags perched atop the spires of skyscrapers make a mockery of the skyscrapers with their indecisive forms.

Second condition: the little masks on the people navigating the canals. Thus, the boats are a mistake. From this height, they are barely visible— images pass. The boats drag the city with them in their deep wakes.

Dear Empire,

These are your countries. Furious sparrows, your citizens bustle about, wanting this and this. To be loved by you.

They've laid out their banners for you, their rugs—fabrics with the sheen of a green serpent's head. When you arrive and wave from the tarmac, lights flare and flare. Each camera flash, a fistful of hearts borne from eye sockets, saying god and god and god.

Everyday they take in your face. Your picture flirts from photo paper in darkrooms, border to border. The cyanotypes muscle out your blue jaw line. Your blue and poisonous eye.

Dear Empire,

These are your docks. Rickety boats clap their sides against tires lining the edges. The rubber chars the sides of the hulls, leaving signatures— streaks of black that rises and falls with the current.

Evenings, fishermen spread their nets to dry. Occasional birds snare legs in the webbing, and the men make a game of it as they toss bits of shell, side-arm at the gulls. Low tide brings the riff-raff beneath the docks, and the heat from their bonfires burn the hairs off the nets' fraying cords. The smell of burning nets and fish scales is elemental— the ocean sets its wild tendrils off into the spray.

Meanwhile, from inside the hulls of the boats, the ocean sounds like a child's stomach. So many hungers fill the open seas.

Dear Empire,

These are your holy places. Your furthest chapel skirts the coasts. Rumors of creatures across the ocean abound. Our children fear to go to the beach.

We have photographed monsters. Note their showcased backs. The two-dimensional images do not do them justice. We carried the head of one of their spies in a lime sack. You like his expression: empty with his gums decaying back into his nostrils.

I fear to tell you something smolders over the horizon. The watch from the chapel tower calls them smokestacks, not monsters. Their spires clutter the once-smooth edge of what you were. Because of this, we've cast the priests from their loft and have lined windows with our top marksmen. Weather balloons jerk with the roiling current. Look to the coast. Take this as a sign.

Dear Empire,

These are your horizons. Endless highways of red soil mix with low, brown clouds. A deep cold. A parched light. It is winter, and fog hangs low in the branches.

On the ground, slivers of frost spike up from the hardened soil. Winter marks its temperament with little crystal swords beneath our feet.

The artist's son rises from the edge of the fog like the far whistle of bird-song. He is an astonishment. The light marvels at the extravagance of his childish body—the only landmark in the flat expanse. The idea of him, here in the barrens. His light hair. His eyes. The audacity of his intrusion in the scene.

Dear Empire,

These are your interstates. Their reach spindles out from the center of the continent, thin strands of roads. Asphalt like magma rays from a central core.

Along the byways, many signs with your brightly lit countenance mark distances. Everywhere we go, you are with us. The mile markers stretch and yaw.

Yellow lines mesmerize drivers; tire treads hum from the wash-boarded roads. In the high deserts, the heat makes the whole scene appear underwater. And the suicides collide with the radiator grills. Your smiling face beams above the sunroofs, into the rearview mirrors. As much as we try to leave you, we keep spooling back.

Dear Empire,

These are your islands. I used to live by the sea. There were monoliths on the shore. Hard currencies of sand dollars brought us an understanding—an answer to our predicaments.

Wave by wave, faces erode—into what? Far from shore, ships idle their motors. The warships are no accident. There are no accidents here.

My memory is sutured shut. The gaps between seams fill with salt. The chitons' plates click together which sounds like marching. Like gathering in a square.

Dear Empire,

These are your maps. All the flotsam shines like lights in the desert.
And here we've buried wires that power your capitals. Here where the
river's silty tongue splits into a fan of tributaries, your gardens.

The dams and levees hold back the floods as you had commanded.
The water is held down like a lunatic. We call it the lunatic's plumage.

And here are your barricades. They displace the horizon just as you
had asked. Each room you've made predictable—the farmlands break
across the plains in tiles. The wheat bows to you. It bends.

Dear Empire,

These are your meadows. They idle, poised with the spring foxglove. Gunpowder black tea steeps in the broth, unfurls in a bouquet of mint.

The artist's son is in the clearing netting monarchs. Both are blossoms rivaling the sky's hue. His net has a snag. It pinches the silken mesh. We have lost our sense of direction.

Glacial ice does not fill the rivers, despite the heat and insects. Corpses in the lake have not brought the water to capacity, and the striations in the stones are dumb to us. There are no more flowers beyond this point.

Dear Empire,

These are your parks. Children kick from swing sets like splendid aerialists. The shadows below them swim to and fro as legs extend and retract. The pendulum of the chains creaks at its hinges.

Some of the boys feign punches and play war games among the planks of the set. Their slow-motion deaths are met with applause as old men watch and feed the geese.

Against the concrete embankments, fliers of your face in a multi-hued display rainbow your countenance. Some of the fliers are torn with age. Some from rain. A child presses his back against the cold cement with his arms up, as the other children make pistols with their fingers, fire, and watch him fall.

Dear Empire,

These are your pastures. Spring brought the goats but no fresh grass for them to graze. Thus, they eat our shirts off the line. We are made nude to sudden downpours. The lapwings wade far from us.

We are clearly a spectacle with no shelter. Thus we are rendered. A distant purr of electrical wire scratches its consent. Beyond, the wading pond fills with bodies of waterfowl.

There are no sounds but the hum and bells at the throats of the goats. The once-thick bramble has been nibbled to spines. We dare not cross the field. We dare not wander.

Dear Empire,

These are your plains. The ranges are laden with snow. All night, horses leave tracks like ellipses, soon covered by drifts at the center of a white page.

I am trying to get this message to you but night is a sealed envelope. I am trying to reach you but the passes are lost and the one star in the sky bites hard into my shoulder.

The freeze is upon us. As I step, the horses jerk their heads back, snap their synapses awake. We are not beyond your jurisdiction. Just in its alcove, soft and muzzle-cold.

Dear Empire,

These are your salt flats. They lie past highways, past towns with gas stations whose names sear the eye in monosyllable and neon. Here, there is nothing except the horizon and the slight curve of the earth.

Tire tracks carve endless signatures—the spasms of giant serpents which wind towards barely visible lights of civilization.

Some mornings, the ocean's breeze meets the heat and lifts off the ground, causing more winds. More dust. Our tracks disappear. There are no animals. No sounds save the sweep of wind or an occasional engine coughing sand. Yet the inhospitableness is their charm. Sometimes it is good to be an erasure.

Dear Empire,

These are your skies. Rivulets write on our cockpit windows, "She is beautiful, and she is sand." The war is contagious. It multiplies like yellow pollen taken into our exhaust when our planes take off. There are names up here—names and the split of light off the glass.

And the rain? What of the rain? It tracks its way, sinuous down the length of the windows. The co-pilot is a bastard for not seeing this.

There is only so much debt my heart can make. I hand myself over to you. I let you ransack. The night is copper, and you are the gleam off the slickened streets in my bombing sites. You are the gleam.

Dear Empire,

These are your springs. The nobles bathe here in winter. Beyond their waters, you cannot see the world—only steam. And when they step naked from the springs, their bodies look on fire.

The lords and ladies are encased in smoke. Their skins break into gooseflesh as they rise, ever so briefly, only to descend again into the hot pools.

The smell of the earth is thick here, like a chemist's residence. Hunks of sulfur cling to rock edges, and the hard egg smell steeps in the hair and clothes. Those who wait on them on the periphery cover their bodies and faces. From the fire. From the ice.

Dear Empire,

This is your tremor. The ground ripples. The ore in the hills flash. Iron like the scales of fish from the stream. There. Then nothing.

Having lost the roads through the mountain, there is no food. I write with a sugar cube disappearing slowly in my mouth.

The city, meanwhile, sinks into chalcedony. We are very small with the backdrop of the decaying hills behind us. There is only the wick of my voice sputtering in the canyon.

Dear Empire,

These are your vistas. The artist takes her palette knife and sharpens the edge of her production. Of the images dedicated to you, this will stand. Clear in the abutment, the sun's angle strikes the mountain precariously.

Shadows drift from the paint's heavy impasto. Perhaps she's covered your face. The insolence of your artisans breaks my heart. As it does yours, I'm sure. All their talk of standards and truth.

Your vistas will be forever with us, I'm sure. The way they resemble your arms. The way their intermediacy shifts the light on everything before them.

Dear Empire,

These are your volcanoes. In the mountains there are caves yet to be found. We feel the wind from their hollows on our faces. I fear falling. I could fall deeply…my body a satellite. Our ropes tremble from gusts deep within.

On the other side, we are sure someone is burning ambassadors. The limestone is hot. It is an ache. We wonder aloud whether you will come. Whether you pray.

We do much to cover our noses from the quick bursts of sulfur fume. Bits of cloth from our old coats, the damp kitchen rags. We can only do so much to heal our throats.

Dear Empire,

This is your wall. On its other side, a courtyard where secrets bloom. Its foundation founders. There are many signs of its near-demise— lichen sprouts like tumors, the graffiti.

Names bubble from its face in cursive tributaries. Hands reach between barbs to grasp a coil from the lowest braid. Along the length of the wall, hands reach up to chip a cake of stone. Edges of rebar, rusty from exposure, pock the wall here and there. Blunt stubble ends. Guards stationed above have guns aimed at the hands. Occasionally they'll fire a round.

Your towers overlook the courtyard. Citizens on the other side of the wall hang small mementos: a twist of hair, a necklace, a bangle. When one looks at the wall from a distance, it is beautiful. A monument of beautiful nerves.

Dear Empire,

These are your wells. Deeply, the pipes tap water up from the silt of the crust. The artist's son's wild hair frets in an ecstatic arc as he runs. His curls in sync with his speed.

All these ideas of him accrue as you watch her watching him. She draws water from a faucet and carries a pail over to where they picnic. She asks him to hold still as she worries the nap on his head with a comb dipped in water.

We have watched these two for some time. Sometimes you wake with an image of yourself. Sometimes trouble falls with each sway of a bucket.

Dear Empire,

These are your wires. They demarcate your borders, of which there are many. And the animals who dare try to cross are shot out of boredom. Here, the dried body of a mule deer turns this way and that. Snow sheaths its form.

We've pulled at its corpse for some time; its hide comes apart in ribbons. Its dried musculature has formed a canvas which we've riddled with bullet holes. Field mice have made a nest of its hairs, and the way the wind whistles through its hollows is a sort of comfort to the men.

Every moon, the deer's ghost is a cluster of notes dancing between the wire's ledger lines. The wind raises and lowers its chords as it wishes.

Ledger

Dear Empire,

This is your aftermath. You were alive after the aftershocks. The long coastal land uncoiled as a rope does when pulled too taut.

There were deerflies around your mouth that carried, on their legs, the taint of someone else's blood. Children were searching for water when they happened upon you, fractured arm of the republics we knew.

Listen, the masses are disconsolate. Comets have foretold your doom. They blaze through evenings like fireflies. We've found you and lost you again, coin of our dwellings—jars of no wheat. Rise . . . rise and shift. Shift and blossom.

Dear Empire,

This is your art. The paintings you ordered destroyed say nothing about you, but about the way the flames licked their frames.

Such a furor arose over the dancer's portrait. Because it is not about love. Because it is language and what the portrait had asked us. Was it your fault that she cried? No, her tears are not your fault.

I held her shoe in the pads of my hands, still warm after she had stepped off stage. There are little ringlets sewn on her dress that resembled fish scales. You should have seen them move. She was like a flash of light on a tiled wall. She was like migration.

Dear Empire,

These are your asylums. Today, the walls have been washed because some men had penned their names in blood and excrement. Bleach now widens the hallways with its odor.

Grime between tiles is another story. Sometimes you find fingernails, hair. Signs other bodies have passed through. They are wild animals— eye sockets, deep with stars and lost potentials.

We keep fighting these ghosts. They keep passing through our walls.

Dear Empire,

These are your banners. Their cloth is the lolling tongues of jackals in heat. High over your stadiums, winds have their way with them. They sway this way and that, click their fabric with each intense gust.

Your subjects below cannot hear words from their own mouths. All sound is chopped to bits by the violence of your symbol.

Here above the summer palaces, your banners drape more tenderly. They do not express themselves with the same gusto as they do over your arenas. Perhaps because of setting or perhaps because of will. There is not so much gravity. There is not so much glory.

Dear Empire,

These are your billboards. They brighten the highways, their panels demarcating a time between longitudes. Time and time—their illuminated marquees strain the power grid's thrumming desires. The signage hums by with their images of smiles, wide as the scaffolds at each base.

Up high, the vector-enlarged faces grid the human. Beauty as proportional as leaves of paper backed by paste and smoothed to a shine. This sign is as simple as the promise it contains. The body of a dancer extends her hands out as a courtesy to you.

This one—an eye that duplicates longing. Whether the eye is blue or green does not matter. Somewhere above the image, the outline of another billboard. Heat from light bulbs ghosts the names beneath.

Dear Empire,

This is your church. Your subjects bow their heads, almost touching the backs of those in front of them. They turn with the vicar's hands, the way faces of flowers move towards sun.

From up close, the vicar's collar has a stain. His voice box strains against its edge.

The high ceilings arch. The burst of a slight cough bounces from one end to the other. Sound keeps all in place. There are blue eyes mounted high above in the leaded windows. Light from them casts down on the heads of those praying. Look, the devout are diving as they bend to pray. They are swept.

Dear Empire,

These are your engines. The weighty ingots held inside the freight cars spark with friction at the sudden stops and starts. There is livestock in the back cars. Dung smells roll forward as the engine slows.

Sometimes there are breaks in the line, and the engineers have to jump from the cab to the ground with shovels, shoeing in the sand and ties before starting again. In times when there is no movement, there is also no sound, save the thud of an animal's tail as it strikes the sides of its carriage.

Today, like every day, the tracks can seize from menace and weather. The black sheen of the rail frames stretches like a spine towards the coast. The animals know some things about where they go. We know they wait for us with their ears to the ground.

Dear Empire,

These are your evenings. The dark has the texture of fur. Fifth floor, the wind vibrates the panes. The signs from the jetty flare and recede. I want to be deliberate but the junctures of the road cannot be seen.

I mailed a letter to you. In this weather, it won't find its way. I said, "Heaven, I was trying to concentrate." I said, "I had meant to be there." Yes, there is more. Yes, this wind is a knife.

The buoy near the furthest atoll is a constant. Red light. None. Red light. None. The boats are moored against their own destruction. They pitch like restless horses. We, from the shore, are nervous. We, from the shore, are listening for the lighthouse. We listen for its shine.

Dear Empire,

These are your foundries. Hot swept bricks outside their doors attract the washer women with their wet linens from the river. All along the corridor, metal pours into forms while women dangle white sheets from the guy-wires used to support the thin roof, dangerously close to the molten metal.

But not a thread of fabric is singed, which must be a trick of magic. The sheets rise up like a choir of ghosts as the machinery guides their leaden wares from point to point.

The cloth curls upward like the flesh of a man on fire. The shriek of gears and joints can be heard from many miles away. Sometimes, you can see blankets sail high above the smokestacks like white-winged gulls.

Dear Empire,

These are your goods. Our baskets are filled with useless gewgaws. A thimble. A handle. A washer. A twist of metal. A spring. Nude, we starve in the jungle as your generals smoke the tobacco we had dried all month.

They've kept some captured monkeys chained to trees. Even more, they've starved them and draw their pistols at their slight protests. There are many manacles dangling from tree limbs. They'd chime if there were a breeze.

Meanwhile, the smoke is no food. Meanwhile we've become feckless without our clothes.

Dear Empire,

These are your guns. They aim elsewhere. Through clouds. Through fog. Elsewhere there are also pine trees. The spines of the needles fall in sharp clouds when it rains. But the artillery does not know this. And therefore, it must be imagined.

Therefore, the artist takes her brush and paints the cliffs in a way that expresses their joy. Therefore the artist sets to make something beyond a paper understanding. To make certain the pines are understood. That the kindnesses of childhood echo in a hail of gunfire.

Yet the tide seeks to take it all back. The passive bodies of jellyfish surrender themselves to movement. To gravity. To life in someone else's music.

Dear Empire,

These are your inquests. We have found evidence scattered throughout the sands, little scabs of metal here and there. Beachcombers slice their feet, making the map of the land a painting wreathed in fury.

And the yellow caution tape clicks its tongues at us. It is a little brat; its ribboning wills stretched out from one end of the beach to the other.

There is no one here to handle the minesweepers. They are afraid, and their emptiness is a domed ceiling. By week's end tides will carry it all out—the blood and the steel. It will look like a mind firing.

Dear Empire,

These are your laws. Having the sharpest eye, the artist had rendered the coast so perfectly; you can see the array of our batteries aimed at the horizon. Delicate and beautiful, blossoms of jellyfish drift in the current below the scene.

And still, if one were to discern our rough terrain, one would take but one look at her careful production and understand the affront of her art. The world is an integral part of its own design—what would the world be without your order? So the law must be written to save the nation. To save us from us.

We have taken her son and his beautiful hair. His skin, the transparent bloom of jellyfish. His skin cool and quaking. The extent of her loss is not known. There are no normal documents rolled out for this. No straight cuts or decrees.

Dear Empire,

This is your light. The generators are silent, private like a cloth over the photos on the mantel. The moon winks as it rains. This night is like the back of a throat. Belladonna black.

Picture, then, the ghost of us. On the ledges, frames back against the table tops. The power grid's gap stretches in longer and longer synapses. For miles, the once-steady gleam of light. Now shadows cast from the lit tapers shift in the wind.

Wax from the house candle drops on the sill, making a jaw shape as it stretches and descends. It sings to no one.

Dear Empire,

These are your mercies. For their sakes, we filled their drinks with poppy milk, their last drinks, cloudy with nectar. And in their delirium, your prisoners were shot in the morning, as the sun cleared the horizon.

You should have seen their ecstatic faces. How their eyes turned inward to read the hollowness of their skulls. Their bodies, rising just slightly with the firing of the guns.

In that instant, all the birds in the courtyard set aloft. Over the precinct, the moon still shows its face in the bright day, pocked by the shadows of birds.

Dear Empire,

These are your murders. I'm not one to speak of atonement, given my sins are expressly for you. Given night's easy wound and your own scar. Given the smell of old papers, the broken figurine you've placed on the mantle. In this humidity, I make the repairs at night. I forget the knick-knacks in my room. It is not a storefront window. It does not light up, and the walls are a problem.

Some days, men sleep beneath my awning on beds of rags. Some days, no rain. The nude reclining is missing his shoulder. Books have fallen from a lack. They lie instead of lean.

When I find the last piece of the man, you will be gone. You will back the car over the gravel. Treads will leave divots in the driveway. I will not wake up, having busied myself all night. The soft ping of a stone from a tire will not stir me. Nor will the record of the body, its hand over its face, the shoulder quite gone.

Dear Empire,

These are your nights. The bats are delicious pirouettes against the moon. We are elemental in the dark. We are out of our skins with our mouths pressed to the ground.

They catch bread we've thrown to the tree branches, and they fall to us with their old faces. My breath is a foot upon my throat as I feel their movement. The skirl of insects covers our trespass.

Meanwhile, there are no mysteries left between us ... only the susurrus wings. Meanwhile there are only furred bodies hurtling through the constellations.

Dear Empire,

These are your orders. They file in from a network of wires over our heads. What time shall I prepare? Shall I be ready?

The control you exert over time has me at zero hour. A null-time. Only the slow drift of a shadow from point A to point B instructs me. Schemes hatch without minds.

In the park, the elderly count the passage of these edicts in their deliberate way. Loaves pass from hands to birds. The sudden strike of a beak on a bare palm.

Dear Empire,

This is your purview. Your general's child is a prat. He talks to stones. He is beyond limbs, beyond lungs. Tell him to stop. He jabs the bitch's teats with a stick and she yelps but tolerates him as if she sees her master's dangling whip.

Tell him to go back. The spring is unnaturally slow, full of fertilizer and the heavy smell of metal. This is no place for insolence.

Fiercer neighborhoods such as these are charmed by patrolmen who carry long poles with a coil of rope at the ends. The boy is in the way of these duties. This is no place for folly. For frolic.

Dear Empire,

These are your processions. Your most famous general had wished to attend the funeral of your most famous artist. Having painted your portrait with a gun to her head, she certainly caught the curve of the occipital bone, the crease under the gunman's eye socket. But it was nothing theatrical.

Regardless, whomever they bury today would have a future that could not offer roses. Her son plays with a tattered curtain from her studio and runs in great velvet arcs about the churchyard.

There is no urn for her ashes. We cannot eat the cake because the frosting is a private color.

Dear Empire,

This is your product. The artist takes her lunches in what's left of the park. All day she spends in the cannery, pressing fruit into thin containers.

She sits inside the empty fountain and unpeels her knapsack. Raw, her gloved hands cannot touch the dried flowers in their beds, else they'll blister.

Once, I walked up to greet her. She held her palm up to say "no." To say "orchid."

Dear Empire,

These are your questions. You fold your hands over a knee as the carriage moves past road reconstruction. Beginning misunderstandings flare like tungsten above our heads.

Therefore, it is considered constantly fashionable to die without ridicule or with palms bare of any callus or scar. Note the workers on the side of the road—how they bear no resemblance to us. To your beautiful hands.

The above must be expressed flatly as to deny one's office. Your hands are beautiful. To deny would simply provoke a question. Such as, "How much do you love me?" Such as, "What is left?"

Dear Empire,

These are your radio towers. With seeming purpose, seeming direction, each slice of air demarcates a zone.

If I were standing on X, I would hear you as clearly as those at Y. There is no silence; the wattage sees to it. From every vantage point, ecstatic tops—red warning lights call their blooms. There are no cadences or coincidences—your voice booms, far beyond innuendo.

On the wires, yellow birds flash. Little muscles. Little breaks in your voice slide into our ears, smoothing their way into a new abode. It sews an order. It sews a hum.

Dear Empire,

These are your ramparts. It is yesterday. It is still yesterday. The machines are at our gate. To see the cogs click against the wheel tracks—I liken it to watching a man being devoured by two tigers.

We've mounted the turrets atop the chimney. That is why sulfur rules the flue and there is no heat. There are also no more revelers in procession, having been unnerved by the continual knock against our buttresses. The candles are running out.

Dearest, our hydrangeas have been ruined by snow. The mirrors in the hallway shake with each crash, making my image ghostly. Forgive my jeremiad. The smoke from the howitzers is a lovely outburst. On that we can agree.

Dear Empire,

This is your reliquary. In this jar, a knucklebone. And here, a skull with gemstones for teeth. The canines of it shine so that light lashes forth. Its smile bends the beams. From it, emerald light strikes the tabernacle. And lo, it too illuminates.

Blessed be those who are smote by the light of its countenance. Blessed be they. As god speaks, the terrible imposition of his glare shuts the eyes of believers settled in the pews.

And here the silver tourniquets of martyrs. Remnants of their collared bodies dangle from the columns of this holy house. This one lacks a femur. His bones fused by wire. And this one's sternum drips with wax. There are candles lit from inside his ribcage. See its light? See how all their bodies glow?

Dear Empire,

This is your sanitarium. The artist had bidden her time here. She had walked the halls with a brush in her hand. She covered the mint-green paint of the walls with bright streaks of vermillion.

Oh, how the shaved heads of the inmates turned to watch as she rushed past with her brushes, heavy and thick with pigment. Her frenzy, her dance, splashed onto the linoleum floors, a bouquet of paint which bore her bright red footprints.

At night, they took her brushes and she could not sleep. Now there are sounds which dominate the cells: a tapping at the walls, the low hum of the men in their beds. The sound of a hand moving from side to side, like swimming.

Dear Empire,

These are your spires. Their girders stretch from ocean to ocean. They form a winking spine. The red light atop each tower strobes our burning thoughts from tip to tip. Enervated. It's as if they are fastidious with their time. They sync their pulses—eye to eye to eye.

No, they keep our time.

From the sky you see them stitch whole scars of terrain. At dawn we see them rise with the wet gloss of the horizon. Their buzz, our cobbled voices. Your oaths, a cold and lustrous hum.

Dear Empire,

These are your squares. Here, they celebrate you under the hard beams of sunlight. There are fists raised. The shadows of fists against the tiles are a mass of black darting fish.

Graffiti streaks the charred surfaces of the walls near places where small bonfires had once stood watch over the sleepers sheltered here for the night. The odor of the corners is ash and cumin. The spice hits your nose as you approach the enclosed areas near the temples.

And when you walk through the center, a rock placed at the center of each tile square commemorates the fallen. It is often hard to walk in these places—the rocks make a constant clicking sound as visitors absently kick them through these vast promenades, and the flash of the blue tile like the glare of the sun off the sea.

Dear Empire,

These are your structures. Your leaders have left us for another continent. Our houses dread the wind, and we are without a scaffold for our things. We hang our coats on nails loosened from the foundation. Our bodies are sidling away while, somewhere, your leaders sip liqueur from coconut husks.

A mist pools at the center of our living room. Perhaps a gas valve is cracked. Perhaps gauze is wrapped around the camera.

The artist says it is the ghost of you. And like other ghosts, there is a hunger for an ellipsis that is necessary.

Dear Empire,

These are your temples. There are rows of stone countenances, pillar after pillar. As if walking through a forest filled with alabaster heads: here, the frown. The gaze. The luminous stare.

Smoke from the incense curls, shapes itself against the archways, rubs against the grooves of the columns. Only a few men press their heads to their hands.

Outside, archeologists excavate a stone torso. Bound in coils of fraying rope, it rises before us, pulled upwards by a backhoe. Its form momentarily hides the sun, though as it sways, the light strikes our eyes. Saying *yes*. Saying *no*.

Dear Empire,

This is your tomb. By coming here, I was hoping for nearness. For a coming back. I am somewhere in the middle.

The guard at the gate takes our money for a map through the graveyard. He's arrogant but lazy, and there are teenagers here, dressed for a parade.

If you crane your neck near these monuments, you can see faces looking back from the sepulcher. Limestone particles pile around the edges of the old tombstones. These dunes shift with each exhalation. Each in-breath. We are breathing in our tributes to the dead.

Dear Empire,

This is your window. Its glass is providential, a form of grief. I see my eye in fragments, reflecting back in the torrential showers. Off the coast, a typhoon dances like a ballerina with her head back and her mouth open.

The rain falls, quicksilver. Out there is an ocean filled with spasms of fish.

The artist cannot paint them because of their movement. "Are they swift?" she asks. "Yes," she answers. "Their swiftness is miraculous."

Dear Empire,

These are your winters. Months from now, the snowdrifts will cover everything in a white residue, muting the hum from the gramophones. Everything will be as through a plastic film.

When the light turns green, I am left with my engine's slow spool. I can hear, or rather, feel, its bass rattle the windows quick, quick-quick, quick. Hardened by the sound, my teeth sets in my jaws.

And beyond it all, your satellites take pictures in space: ice craters upon ice craters, a comet's tiny body hurtling in orbit through space. Your satellites are in constellational drift—gods launched into the ether, their limbs moving in orbit. They watch us all, I think. I think I am constantly judged by you.

Zoo

Dear Empire,

These are your aerialists. The peals of thunder we hear on a clear day startle all the livestock. The cattle barrel into the fences despite the electrical wire.

And despite ourselves, we flinch as they approach, low to the ground and fast as sparrows. The children below the jets plug their ears and flinch. We see the contrails rake white lines across the sky as though someone had run a finger through limns of a painting.

Against our hearts we feel their approach. Here they come again. Here they are.

Dear Empire,

This is your assembly. Women in green queue to the left. There, they are cordoned by your officers in naval white. They all stand at attention. Stock still like the one foot of the crane that steadies its body aloft.

Men are held back by your officer's bodies, linked arm in arm. The men in blue work clothes are hard to distinguish from the women, save the severe white line they've formed. Like teeth. Like exaggerated canines.

A simple gesture, at this time, would telegraph movement, and this human painting would dissolve. Thus the record player throws its voice in allegro to help the march. Your soldiers hold them back. Keep the time.

Dear Empire,

These are your beasts. We have gathered all the pets from the remaining houses. It is a gray day that will have us do this. We breathe heavily because our nostrils are stuffed with torn strips of clothing.

Our fingernails are dark with oils and blood. Your edict is firm and true. And what we do, we do with full sorrow.

Someone has left a dish besides the window. Calcium and salts ring its rim. Asides from the dish, nothing except dark hairs piled into the corners and the nail scratches on the floorboards.

Dear Empire,

This is your bestiary. The book urges a soft breeze from its pages as a hand riffles from the back to the front. Here the ink labors with the pictures of sea creatures, scales, and crepuscular things glowing in the near dark.

And here, the artist's madness settles in her shaking hand. Here are birds, and here the hooved animals moving in a herd. Their pastures are secrets to anyone but themselves, and they run to them, hearts gassed on the veneer of their instincts.

And here are the homonids. This one bares your face. This one is the artist. See them dance as the pages turn. See them break in the sweep of paper.

Dear Empire,

These are your birds. The geese fly their commutes, one calling ahead. Others join the storm of voices. From border to border, they are still yours.

And below, your map's lines delineate climes: sassafras, estuary, depot. The hum of a blade through a beak, through a throat. The taste of eelgrass, changed. The hard edges of a weary wing. In books, your artist cataloged them all because you loved them. Because of how much you longed.

It takes the birds seven days to get any place. Their migrations are the long and vegetal climb back into the body. For you, there is the constant nag of nest.

Dear Empire,

These are your bondsmen. We see them come from high mountains in caravans of shawls and ragged hats. They wear their bedrolls on their backs and descend like strange dromedaries as they crisscross down the trails made by the goats.

The bright red coffee cherries, when plucked, are hardened knuckles. The baskets slung low from shoulder to waist, shake as the pickers step from bramble to bramble. To hear it, one would think of rain—the beans like the pitch of a storm.

It would amuse you to watch them move, the pickers. Like watching animals climb bramble, high above the jungle canopies—one hand crosses another, snaps back the terrible stems.

Dear Empire,

These are your dead. They are buried above ground, so it is hard to say they are buried. Often, they are among us: a parasol on a sunny day, a partnerless shoe.

Lupine shudder with every gust. Their purple buds thread up like kitchen brushes from the graves. There are many gardens here. There are many feet wearing uneven treads on the soil.

If you took a photo negative of me right now, you would see the heat outlines of ghosts. The upright caskets are violent with their exhaust. This is me placing flowers on a stone. This is me beside the wisteria, twisted around the gate's trellis. These are your solar flares.

Dear Empire,

These are your devotees. From their mouths, hail pours into hail. The real misfortune of knowing them is their understanding of your game. Their minds are verbs, and upon the land they happen in avalanches over your governed.

Which is why you love them. The way they sound alike. The way they move their eyes and thus control what they see. All those twitching satellites before them are also yours, and it's easy work for you because of what they do.

What little monsters you have made. They favor you. They draw your praise.

Dear Empire,

These are your dissidents. They are dark and threadbare like the stripped corpses of trees in winter. They feather the hillsides in their cloth houses. Whole hillsides are awash in bright fabric—riverbeds of canvas.

At night, the valley is a galaxy of small fires. There are songs that can be heard above the shelling in the distance. Sometimes the thuds are percussion for their songs.

This year is growing long, and the ravines have lost their grasses. What shall we do? The winter rains will wash them out as one sweeps bits of dust to the floor. What shall we do with these bodies at the gate?

Dear Empire,

These are your followers. There are many dogs here with the names of dictators. The children tease them with sharp sticks. I watched one bitch collie chase its wounded hind leg until it expired from exhaustion. The streets need sweeping.

Thank you, by the way. The wine you sent does not age, despite its lack of a cork. I am reminded of the old distilleries from my youth, where rows of pinot noir were each eclipsed by the slight shade of the morning hillsides. These mortals certainly do not understand us.

Despite the putrefaction in these streets, I want to say how much your goodwill is welcome. I cask it. I cask you from far away.

Dear Empire,

These are your hagiographers. Of the growing squall, they write little. Their pens are bright flights on the skeins of skins. Bade, as they are, to scribe your will—your thirst so tethered to circling hawks and up-coming irises. Tethered to the potentials.

Because the history of us is your thirst. Imagine, the locked gates of the tomb or of the mind's spangled phantoms—also you.

August, September, October, such a high violence flushed by the lambent edges of quills.

Dear Empire,

These are your horses. They hurt to watch, scarring the prairie as they do. The way they draw north or heed your call and cross the river, even when it is far too high.

See their heads jut just above the water? How quickly the small ones drown. How tame they are as they tire. Their skins absolve you of their aches, being beautiful.

Their eyes rise and surge. They break as easily as men do, lacquered, blooming. Hearts full of anticipatory pastures.

Dear Empire,

These are your idolaters. They carry you in chains around their necks. Your graven images spark the air. At night, they fling their lamps on the way to their churches, and the light that passes between faces becomes a relation. Like a new language passed between, as if by accident.

As if by accumulation we come to god.

Among them, there are particulate stars moving about. Sparks from the lamps and the rebound from the gilded chains. How beautiful it is. The sense that your face creates stars. The sense that your face creates a becoming. A pronouncement.

Dear Empire,

These are your jellyfish. They are the artist's obsession. The way their forms are taken by tides. Pulled towards the shore or towards some unknowing place. Our beaches are cursed by thousands of these little ghosts.

Yet she fills her canvases with their clear and brilliant orbs. Occasional tendrils seem to slide off the edge. Their little hidden fires. Their little underneath parts papering the dark.

To have a mind as hers. To have an eye that understands the little shocks beneath. To consider that these ghosts have such an edge. Such a sting.

Dear Empire,

These are your nurseries. The orphans here are divided into rows according to time of their birth. They are arranged alphabetically, so as not to lose track of them.

Little blue and pink shoots scoot back and forth in incubators. The nurses pace with their hair tied up. Masks cover their faces. Their eyes shift from bed to bed.

The hum of the air conditioning is audible above the cries of the children, and you can see small fingers rise from the swaddles. Some of the children raise voices. Some of them hold still.

Dear Empire,

These are your orators. Shined up, they line amphitheaters with their brilliant stupefactions. A sequence of incongruities streams from their tongues, silvered and rich.

Sweet devils, their vowels uncurl in lariats of errata. Every ear can be bought, they say, each price to be named as the globe turns on its hinge. Of course, we must pity the gullible boys whose faces alight like the roundest fluorescence to their silken call.

These spectators become your hardiest enervations. From their mislaid memories comes your grasp. Come your rhetorical hammers.

Dear Empire,

These are your percussionists. On the ground, we feel the roll of their approach. Treads turn the dirt in a succession of rat-at-ats.

Every so often the heavy bass of a turret fires a shell into a stuccoed wall. And the earth stirs with machinery in the dark. We hear their engines drive the vast mesas; the tinnier sound of their metal plates a high metronomic pulse against the drone of their motors.

We wait for their approach. We are the silence that multiplies itself in the night. We are the dark with our eyes closed. We are the hard knots pressed against the drum.

Dear Empire,

These are your phantoms. Clothes hang from windows as ghosts of this city. The weather is a mistake. It shakes the forms above the street, fills them. Empties.

The artist asks to be taken to shelter. She hands me sweetbread, as if to spite the hanging ghosts. The edge of her index finger is calloused from holding camel hair brushes and from canning food. As the loaf passes between us, the hardened skin makes a sound on the crust.

Let me say that, despite the artist, I am tired of this city. Its obscene ghosts. Let me say that some of this is your fault. That the lines parallel above our heads are nerve endings. Each push of wind is a message—a movement.

Dear Empire,

These are your rebels. Their wills fill the edge of a pit. They are teeth, throats, the sudden sable plume of a feather from a helmet. They meet in old houses whose walls were once doors.

The floors, once a broken field of stones. And now blue ceilings. Now the smell of orange peel sprayed on the bodies in repose.

The artist paints the rebels to music as they cross the bridge to your battlements. A small steamer announces itself in grand orchestrations over a pit soon to be turned to a tomb. In the scene, the artist paints flowers, the slow canal in front of rows of conifers, and not the awkward deaths in the pit. Because of a forced perspective. Because of the way she succumbs to the song.

Dear Empire,

These are your refugees. The tents they use to cover their heads are made of a soft, translucent fabric. When winds spill from down the mountain, the tents inflate like the sails of a ship. The whole valley is adrift in an arid sea. And when the sun strikes the tents, you see the shadows of the people against the rippling curtains of silk:

Here is a family, the silhouette of the mother is turned to one side, then disappears as the walls of the tent fold inward. And here is a child with a ball. Here is an old woman with her back pressed against the walls of cloth, craning her head as though she were listening to music from beyond the camp. As though she were filled with the expectation of water in a very hot month.

From the mountains above the camp, the tents are the egg sack of a giant amphibian, the living hearts beating clear in a clutch of embryos.

Dear Empire,

These are your revelers. They've pulled acetate from video cassettes and are running through streets with their arms full of these streamers. And the cellulose shines in almighty colors in the sunlight. The cellulose swallows the din of their joy. Nothing like this will last. To dream en masse like this is to watch the ramparts blaze.

To dream as the revelers pour pass the state houses and past the human debris is to watch the oxidation of the Empire happen overnight.

This will not happen to you. The world is full of dreams spinning around their reels. In this cell, a man lifts a glass. In this cell, he is still lifting a glass. In this cell, there is a hand on a glass, and the glass rises.

Dear Empire,

This is your rival. He counts the heads of the prisoners while peeling rinds of oranges with his fingernail. Fruits unravel, their skins uncoiling in one continuous strand. When he passes the antechamber, the smell of citrus is a palpable ghost.

Oh, to be a part of his ghostly orchard! At the feet of his throne rest the bright snakes of his accounting. Were I a herpetologist, I'd classify the fruit serpents as a new species; I'd name a new industry. These are dark fragrances.

The coffiner is counting the coins in his pocket. The smell of his hands is acidic and burns my eyes.

Dear Empire,

These are your scholars. In their presence, the story is a bird, shot through. The stone of the sling passes through its chest taking with it the heart in a dazzling array of blood. In their presence, the blood sticks to everyone's clothes.

Because the story is a sequence of projectiles, someone is liable to be struck. And the profundities of your rule are little gods. Facts rain down like the casing from a fired gun. Hollow jackets clang against pavement, and the ring of their emptiness encumbers the ear.

We are ever wary of their direction. We are ever careful of their trajectories.

Dear Empire,

These are your scribes. The sound of your voice from the reel-to-reel tape travels in spirals, translucent. The synchronic hiss of the acetate is like the clapper of a temple bell—sound of the hard ridges of a dragonfly wing as it slaps against glass.

A scribe's job of translating internal phenomena into decree is akin to your dancer spilling her form as the music stops. As her feet trace the edge of the floor in silence. During winter, the tables are cold and the cyan of the ink turns a dark and viscous black. The writing feathers out, as the skill of the writers fail. There are waves in their handwriting because of weather. Because of fatigue.

You are dictating in a far off place. Your mouth is adjacent to the microphone. The texture of your voice, as painful as particulates in the air.

Dear Empire,

These are your stables. You must make an argument for their form. The horses within are lined from head to tail like a single organism—muscles and hearts, a sinuous machine.

The stable boys are commoners from the street. See how they have no shirts, save the ones we've given them? Dare we let them touch your beasts with their hands the way they are? Dare we be casual with their unknotting of the bluest tendon?

See how they brush the horses' sides? See the sparks of static in the dark?

Dear Empire,

This is your stevedore. She is worthless. She cannot lift a thing, let alone the cargo I bring you. Her arms are lifeless jellies. Her wrists, limp with silver bands.

Fire your gypsy. She stares and stares at blank canvas all day, and when it comes to actual work her body dangles.

Though she is lovely, she has the worth of poetry. There is a distant jangle in her eyes that makes her step uneven with the dock's pathways. She will lose your casks to the sea. She will flash a knife at you, pulled from her boot, as you try to touch her red hair.

Dear Empire,

This is your subject. The artist's son spends the day at the ruins of the aquarium. The boy's hair is a mess, a thicket of tangles. We watch him discover the bones of groupers, bass, the harsh jaw of the barracuda.

His body is thin from a diet of grasses and decomposing fish. His own bones, a jangle of keys. He pursues what's left of the porpoises—the one remaining living tank.

They gun from end to end in unison: one sleek, the other, a spasm of skin.

Dear Empire,

These are your slaves. Their smiles are charcoal and fiber. Their smiles are the sharpest machete. Here, they bend with their backs like bright wet stones in the fading sun. Here they grasp the cane in their fists and swing their blades. And here is where they wade into the husks with torches.

Then the fire. The hairs of the dried cane leaves blacken, then curl into a diminishing crescents.

Snakes in the periphery spill out of the tall grasses like a lambent stream. In the glow of the fire, the sugar men are a wild joy with their hats rising from the gusts of hot air. Funny devils. See them dance among the snakes and the burning sugar, chasing their thin straw hats?

Dear Empire,

This is your ward. His hair curls like solar flares. He is insolent about you, though he hides his fires within. The drawings he makes are rubbed raw against his palm edge, and when you see him, forgive the redness of his palms.

Forgive the young. He is not broken. His heart is improbable...cleaved yet not fooled by anything he has seen. He has an artist's eye—an ability to trim the edge of any design. To see pattern before it unfolds.

And, therefore, he is our doom. Fanatics can be bred from indigents. Fanatics can only ration the now. This one adores the past. Adores lost centuries. Adores foundations from the oldest brick wall.

Dear Empire,

These are your witnesses. They walk with hoods over their heads, and we can only see their mouths. They dart in and out of the traffic, which slows your city to a thrombic buzz. Arms and shoulders bump into the vendors' carts as they hurry out of daylight's gaze.

If you're patient, you can see an occasional foot rise from under their tunics. The heavy sole of their boots grip the dirty streets, leave crossing rows of chevrons here and there until carts smear down the dust.

They will be found out. There are corners in your city where the tongues from the walls can be paid with merely food and drink. There are couriers darting about with knives tucked in their socks. The city is full of windows, bright and yawning.

Dear Empire,

These are your worshippers. They dye their tunics in the river in buckets full of mashed flowers and spice. Others congregate in circles around small fires.

The air here is filled with smoke, scented with funerary ash. Sometimes the river overruns the levees and its water turns to rust.

Tangled in its drag, the holy men mark their foreheads with turmeric powder. Their yellowed heads drift in the current like notes from a car's passing horn.

Dear Empire,

These are your zebras. What an odd thing to bring to your lands, but what an extravagance. There is power, and there is power. Upon the plains, the herds churn dust clouds seen hundreds of miles away.

Your legislators idle in your reserves for sport. Look, they pose for the camera. At their feet, one of the beasts. Its tongue hangs from the side of his mouth, and its eyes stare behind at the tall savannah grasses. At the shiny boots.

You've said before that you would like to keep us happy. A horizon forms around your voice. The plane of who you are separates into different spaces. The striped ribs of the zebra slowly rise and fall.

Zygote

Dear Empire,

This is your photo. It is absent of flowers. In your left hand, your thumb and no oxeye daisy. You hold no stamens. No flora. The generals made in your image face the other direction. So let the forgetting begin with the index finger.

In your right, you hold nothing except the nearest sea behind. Thus, no rain. Thus the disappearance of asters in smoke. And in the darkness of the sea, something blooms. Something blooms. Something unseen divides and rises. Millions of medusa polyps burst beneath the tides. Millions of mindless mouths at your back.

The weight of your body compresses the sea. The sea with its mouths despite a battery of howitzers aimed beyond you. You make an indentation. You make a cavern of you.